WHO MOVED THE GOALPOST?

SEVEN WINNING STRATEGIES IN THE SEXUAL INTEGRITY GAME PLAN

An active, Bible-based curriculum for young men

A ten-session retreat or ten-week Bible study

To be used with the book
Who Moved the Goalpost?
by Bob Gresh with Dannah Gresh

BY BOB AND DANNAH GRESH

ISBN: 0-8024-8338-0

1 3 5 7 9 10 8 6 4 2

Printed in the United States of America

contents

INTRODUCTION
A WORD FROM **BOB GRESH**

the need

So, you're ready to take on the task of teaching young men to live lives of sexual integrity. Have you really thought about this? I mean, isn't that a lot like finding a needle in a haystack? Just look at the stats:

- *Forty-three percent of conservative Christian teenagers say they have had sex by age eighteen.* That is, full-fledged sexual intercourse. It doesn't take into account the rapid rise in oral sex, mutual masturbation, and other forms of sexual contact.
- *Approximately 64 percent of Christian men struggle with sexual* addiction *or* compulsion, *which might include pornography, compulsive masturbation, or other secret sexual activities.* That's the information we have on adult men. Though I have yet to find a comprehensive survey on teen guys and sexual compulsions, most of the adults say it started during their teen years. It just never went away. At one Promise Keepers event, half of the men present said they'd viewed pornography in the week preceding the event. Pornography is deeply affecting our church, and the problem is growing at a rapid rate. If we want to fight the effects of pornography, we've got to start where it begins to take root . . . during the teen years.
- *A survey of college men found that 88 percent of them had masturbated at least once.* The joke I keep hearing is that the other 12 percent are lying. If you're a guy, you can probably relate to the great conflicted emotions masturbation presents.

The problem is big. I truly believe that it is the strongest force fighting against a guy's ability to have a healthy relationship with Jesus Christ. That's why I think it's so worthwhile to take it on face-to-face. Do I feel adequate to the task? No. And you may not either. I'm still trying to find the man who's mastered his sexual passions perfectly. But step up to the plate with me anyway. Let's see what God does, not only through us, but in us as we seek to take the lead in the battle against lust.

Who Moved the Goalpost? The Leader's Guide provides all the creative ideas, research, and planning you need to present a fun and deeply challenging two-day, one-night retreat. (Or you may opt to use it as a ten-week Bible study.) The most powerful portions of *Who Moved the Goalpost?* are presented in this active learning curriculum using small group discussions, individual activities, group games, and fun object lessons. Every session carries a deep scriptural challenge to the guys on a comfortable, approachable level.

our objectives

The retreat's primary purpose is to give young men practical tools to live a life of purity. Our objectives are simple but powerful. The young men who attend will:

- Recognize that "you are not alone" in your struggle against lust.
- Learn that the issue of sexual purity is a lifelong journey and it won't "go away when I'm married."
- Identify the difference between being innocent and being pure.
- Establish informal mentorships with men who participate as groups leaders.
- Recognize the covenant purpose of sex as well as the earthly blessings that God rewards us with if that covenant is protected.
- Establish boundaries to avoid enticement and muscle memory triggers that arouse desires to masturbate, view pornography, or act out sexually.
- Establish specific boundaries to avoid sexual contact with young women.
- Witness the emotional turmoil girls face for what may be a lifetime when exposed to sexual sin.
- Learn the difference between shame and guilt, and begin to embrace God's grace.

our methods

Think back to the important things you've learned. Chances are, you learned by experience. My educational philosophy is that the most effective kind of learning is experiential. The least effective kind of learning comes from verbal teaching. I believe in active learning. (And I fall asleep when I'm not learning that way!) Everything you do with this curriculum has the intended purpose of teaching . . . even playing Maul Ball! (If only all learning were this fun!) The verbal teaching will be supported by simple experiential options. Simply offering the guys a Slinky to play with at the end of Session Two when we talk about the spiral of life embeds that image into their minds and gives them something experiential to attach the truths to.

This curriculum uses three types of sessions, which emphasize experiential learning with limited verbal teaching. The three types of sessions are:

- **Alone Time**— A great risk to sexually addictive or compulsive men is quiet. They have never learned to be OK with who they are in the stillness, and so often find that quiet time is a risk. On the other hand, great men of the faith such as the apostle Paul, C. S. Lewis, D. L. Moody, and others embraced solitude as evidenced by endless journal entries and writings produced in solitude. The guys at your event need to learn to embrace quiet. So, we'll give them a few chances to write in journals or on notebook paper or to read their Bibles and their own personal copy of *Who Moved the Goalpost?* Don't be intimidated by this time. It's important.

- **Small Group Time**—I really want these guys to connect to one of the adult men you select to attend as small group leaders. Many of the sessions require discussion and games. We'll do this in small groups so they have a better chance of interacting one-on-one with one adult male who really wants to help them live a life of purity. Aside from God's presence at this event (or Bible study series), the mentors are the most powerful factor. Select these men carefully. There should be one for every five to ten young men attending.
- **Large Group Challenges**—This is when some verbal challenges will take place, but even these sessions are often very interactive, requiring some careful planning to prepare. Take time to read ahead and be ready.

Thanks for stepping up to the plate with me. I'm certain that God will do some great things.

And . . . by the way, watch out for that goalpost!

what you need

This guide gives you all the information you need to conduct a great event. In each session, you will have items that you need to secure for the lesson. Here are a few of the main items you need to order ahead of time. Purchasing these is strongly advised:

- Focus on the Family's "No Apologies" video
  Call 1-800-A-FAMILY.
- One copy of *Who Moved the Goalpost?* for each leader and attendee
  Call 1-800-678-6928.

getting ready

- **Plan your publicity** well in advance using the publicity materials and ideas beginning on page 47.
- **Gather a minimum of ten men to pray.** These men must commit to pray daily prior to and throughout your event. You might also ask the mothers of the guys attending to pray. Mother's prayers are powerful. If you are conducting this as a ten-week Bible study, ask the mothers to pray throughout the ten weeks, but especially on the days you meet. This is a vital part of your planning. If you don't cover your event in prayer, don't expect God to do much. Be prepared for the blessing if you do pray.
- **Gather one adult small group leader for every five to ten attendees.** This needs to be an older, wiser man who will attend and be involved with the guys who participate. His heart should be open to continuing a mentoring relationship with any of the guys who are open to that idea. He'll meet with you once to get an overview, but the small group guide sheet will carry him through each session quite easily, so his preparation time will be minimal. However, you may want to provide a copy of this guide to each small group leader, and you can always opt to have them tackle leading a session or two.

Select your small group leaders carefully and with much prayer. Like I said earlier, I have yet to meet the guy who has truly mastered his sexual passions, but these small group leaders need to be striving for that.

how to use this guide

To get started, read the brief overview at the beginning of each session. This overview will include the objective of the session, the action to be undertaken by each attendee, the items needed, and the preparation activities that you must tackle. If you are planning this as a retreat, you will want to do this several weeks in advance so you can enjoy the planning and take your time. If you are planning this as a ten-week Bible study, you should still read through the overviews collectively several weeks in advance so you can plan ahead for items that require some time to allocate.

As you plan more in depth for each session, you will see that you can read through it and easily facilitate the session. For the speaking sessions, the session is written for you as you would speak it. These are your speaking notes. Just highlight, write in the margin, have these with you; and you are ready to go. Here are some other helpful hints as you plan:

• Each session is designed to be approximately one hour in length. (If you are doing it as a ten-week Bible study, schedule an hour and a half so you have time to socialize.) You can modify that as you see fit for your group. Once you add in snack times, meals, and free time, the retreat is about fifteen hours, excluding sleep time.

• Dive in and participate, and make sure that your small group leaders do, too. Don't be spectators. This will make it more fun for you and more effective for the young men who attend.

• Don't tell attendees in advance what you have planned. Keep everything as a surprise. Sometimes we'll push you out of your comfort zone to act silly, but everyone will enjoy it and learn. Active learning isn't always comfortable but it is memorable.

• Sources used in the stats section:

Josh McDowell and Bob Hostettler, *Right from Wrong* (Word, 1994).
Patrick A. Means, *Men's Secret Wars* (Grand Rapids: Revell, 1996).
Laurie Hall, *An Affair of the Mind* (Colorado Springs: Focus on the Family, 1996).
Lelan Elliot and Cynthia Brantley, *Sex on Campus* (New York: Random, 1997).

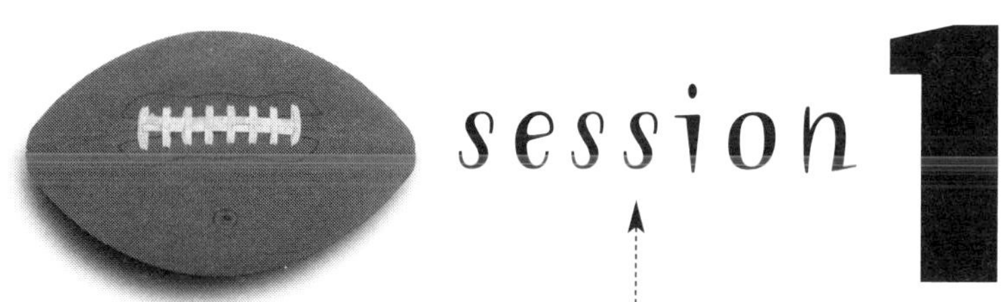

session 1

WHO MOVED THE GOALPOST?

objective:
To introduce attendees to the concept that "you are not alone."

action:
To play Modified Maul Ball.

items needed:
One football
Four orange cones
A football field (optional)

preparation activities:
Read chapters 1, 2, 3, 4 in *Who Moved the Goalpost?*

SESSION 1 AT A GLANCE

ACTIVITY	MINUTES	WHAT ATTENDEES DO
Game Time	*15*	*Play the regular version of Maul Ball*
Challenge	*15*	*Hear proof that "you're not alone" in your struggle*
Game Time	*20*	*Play Modified Maul Ball*
Challenge	*10*	*Wrap up*

lesson at a glance

This is perhaps the most important session. You'll set the tone for your entire event or series here. But relax! This is also one of the easiest sessions. You and your team of mentors simply need to be ready to have fun with the guys in this session.

The greatest challenge for you in this session is comfortably using some language to break the ice. If you can't comfortably say "masturbation," "sexual intercourse," "fondling of the breasts," and so forth, you'll simply add to the broken perception the church feeds young people about sexuality. It's time to change that. For this session, pray hard, and present powerfully and confidently.

welcome/
game time

Welcome/Game Time
Maul Ball • 15 Minutes
You've probably played Maul Ball some time in your life. But just to refresh your memory or in case your version is somewhat crazy, here's how it works.

1. Use a football field for effect if you can. In the field or in a large marked field or gymnasium, mark two "end zones" with your cones. The cones will also establish your field boundaries. The smaller the field, the better, as it will magnify the effect of the modification in just a few minutes.

2. Instruct your attendees and the mentors that you'll be playing Maul Ball. Here are the rules:

- One person will close his eyes at "midfield" and throw the ball into the air after being spun around several times so he does not know in which direction he may be throwing.
- All of the other guys, who should spread out prior to the throw, will attempt to gain control of the ball. The one who gets the ball will attempt to run it in for a touchdown in either direction. He is a one-man team. No one will assist. He must stay within the boundaries established before the game.
- All of the other guys are now playing defense and will do anything to tackle (or maul) the one-man offense.
- When the one-man offense is effectively "mauled," he will spin and throw the ball from that position.
- Continue the game for several rounds, keeping score if you want to.

3. When about fifteen minutes are up and the guys are really into destroying one another, ask them to take a break while you introduce the key concept of the weekend. They'll get to play more Maul Ball in a short while.

large
group
challenge

Large Group Challenge
You're Not Alone • 15 Minutes
Remember, during the challenge sessions or whenever you see italics, these are your speaking notes. Just highlight or add notes in the margins and you are ready to go.

We're going to have a great weekend and I think we're off to a great start with Maul Ball, but I'm going to change the rules to the game. I think you'll see that sometimes changing the game can be good.

Take, for example, the game plan of sexual integrity. But before we plan a strategy against Satan's tactics, I think we should look at how the church addresses the game. Let me fuel your thoughts with Bob Gresh's Who Moved the Goalpost? Seven Winning Strategies in the Sexual Integrity Game Plan. *He writes:*

(Read from "Once upon a time there was a man . . ." on page 30 to the small bold letters ending with "Thou-shalt-nots" on page 32.)

The church could use a new game plan, and that's why we're here this weekend. We're here to speak out and to speak truthfully about the "alligator" of sexual sin.

Of course, while the church is ignoring the subject, Satan, the opponent, is out there playing hard. Sometimes you might feel like his personal pawn in a nasty version of Smack Down. His lies are powerful and destructive to a guy wanting to play by God's rules. What are some of the sex lies you think Satan throws at you?

(Let them share a few. Stay on schedule, but use this time to briefly let them interact. They'll tend to select "safe" lies to share such as "Everyone's doing it." "A condom can make sex safe." Your job will be to make the lies more personal.)

Has anyone ever felt like sex is a four-letter word? Something not to be spoken of? When? What made you feel this way? Why?

OK, let me ask you something really personal since we're just getting it all out on the table today. You don't have to raise your hands or acknowledge an answer. I'd prefer right now that you didn't. But answer honestly in your heart.

- *Have you ever felt like you are all alone?*
- *Feel like you are the only one struggling with, say, masturbation?*

  Guess what. One college survey said that 88 percent of guys reported struggling with masturbation. The big joke? The rest must be lying!

  YOU ARE NOT ALONE!!
- *Have you ever felt like no other guy in this group could possibly be looking at pornography?*

  Here's a mindblower. At one Promise Keepers event, 50 percent of the men attending reported having viewed pornography during the week leading up to the event! Guess what.

  YOU ARE NOT ALONE!!
- *Do you feel like you might be the only one struggling with daily sexual thoughts?*

  There's another college survey that stated that 54 percent of men thought about sex daily—a number that caused humorist Dave Barry to conclude, "The other 46 percent of the men are lying. Because it's a known scientific fact that all men think about sex a minimum of all of the time!"

  YOU ARE NOT ALONE!!
- *Are you struggling and feeling all alone because of outright sexual sin in your life?*

  A recent study of Christian teens showed that 43 percent had experienced sexual intercourse by age eighteen. That doesn't include those who have engaged in fondling of the breasts or genitals or other sexual exploration. If you've struggled in this way, I have a message for you . . .

  YOU ARE NOT ALONE!!!

  Don't get me wrong! I'm not saying these things are OK. ***They are not OK!*** The Message *version of the Bible puts it this way in Ephesians 5:11–14 when it says, "Don't* *waste your time on . . . the barren pursuits of darkness. Expose these things for the sham they are. It's a scandal when people waste their lives on things they* ***must do in the darkness*** *where no one will see. Rip the cover off those frauds and see how attractive they look in the light of Christ"* (emphasis added).

This weekend, we're going to come out of the darkness. We're going to stop playing the game of sexual integrity alone. And that may mean changing the game a bit.
In fact, let's just see what happens when we change the game a bit.

game time

Game Time
Modified Mall Ball • 20 Minutes
Restart the game of Maul Ball but modify it according to these directions with each new round.

1. Ask the guys to partner up with someone they've never met or don't know that well. They may work any way they like as a team. Try to get one team to score or give them three to five minutes to play like this. When a team catches the ball, they work together while those who do not catch it are again one massive line of defense.

2. Ask each team to select another team to work with so you now have teams of four working together. Try to get one team to score, or give them three to five minutes to play like this.

3. Have your teams of four join into teams of eight or twelve if you have enough to do this. Try to get one team to score playing this way before you end the game.

Large Group Challenge • Wrap-up • 10 Minutes
So, was it easier to score or gain yards by yourself or with a team? (Give them a chance to offer feedback.) What happened as you added players? Now, imagine that your opponent is Satan himself and he's trying to cheat you out of winning one of God's most fantastic blessings. How would you want to play? Would you choose to be all alone? Or would you want to be on the team? Know this . . . YOU ARE NOT ALONE! So, you might as well play as if you are not alone. That's what this weekend is about.

We may even change a few other rules of the game as we go along. That's what Who Moved the Goalpost? *is all about. Let me read to you what Bob writes about the goalpost.* (Read Chapter 1, page 13 beginning at the word "bammm!" to the end of the page.) *What are some of the "goalposts" of sexual integrity that you run into? Things that really make it hard to run across that victory line? For example, a goalpost of mine is* (INSERT YOUR EXAMPLE HERE. Invite the guys to offer some of theirs. Have the mentors ready to offer some if the guys don't. This can be a slow process. Be patient.) *It's a tough contest, but together we can win. Let's ask God to coach us through this.*

(Close the session in prayer.)

session 2

CLIMBING THE SPIRAL MOUNTAIN

objective:

To define purity and to differentiate it from innocence.

action:

To draw a picture of the thing that most keeps each of them from pursuing purity in his life and to place that at the cross of Jesus.

items needed:

A large bundle of pens or pick-up sticks
A Slinky for each guy (optional)
A large poster board
One large roll of poster paper for each fifteen guys and colored markers

preparation activities:

Read over the presentation text. You will teach a lesson in this session.
Read chapter 6 in *Who Moved the Goalpost?*
Prepare the poster board with a visual similar to that found on page 61 in *Goalpost.*

lesson at a glance

SESSION 2 AT A GLANCE		
ACTIVITY	**MINUTES**	**WHAT ATTENDEES DO**
Game Time	*10*	*Play "Chinese Numbers" to learn to look past the obvious*
Challenge	*25*	*Learn a three-step definition of purity*
Alone Time	*10*	*Draw graffiti representing their struggle with lust vs. purity*
Small group	*15*	*Receive affirmation from small group leaders*

game time

Game Time

Chinese Numbers • 10 Minutes

Chinese numbers is a game that teaches us to look beyond the obvious . . . to think outside of the box. It's a mind-bender I've used in the adult corporate setting, and it can have maddening results as it wakes up the mind of your audience. With your bundle of pens or pick-up sticks in hand, tell the guys you are going to make a "Chinese" number on the floor, being careful not to say that you will be using your bundle of pens or pick-up sticks. They are to guess what the number is as they discover how the numbers are made. They should not tell the others how it is done. (Give them time to discover it. Be patient. It takes a while.) To make a number, carefully lay four to ten pens in a Chinese-number-looking pattern. Then, subtly lay your hands to the sides of the pattern on the floor so that all of the guys can see them. You will be making the actual number with the number of fingers you have extended. If you want to make a three, lay three fingers casually on the floor with the rest curled under your hand. Let them guess what your Chinese number is. After a few numbers, give them the clue that "I am incapable of making a number higher than ten." As the guys begin to get it, invite them to make numbers for the group, taking turns so that several of them get to try. Toward the end of your time limit, take over again. Some of them will still have not gotten it. This time, be clumsy and drop the pens onto the floor and obviously place your fingers next to the numbers. Make sure that each of them sees how it has been done, explaining it if needed. End by saying, "Sometimes you have to look beyond the obvious for the truth of a situation. Let's see if we can do that right now with the subject of sexual integrity."

large group challenge

Large Group Challenge

Can I ask you something? Do you ever feel like your spiritual life is an out-of-control roller coaster? One day you're reaching upward and moving on toward a great relationship with God and the next you're in total free fall? I've felt that way. It can really make you feel ruined and inferior in your walk with Christ, especially when the cause of the free fall is sexual sin.

I went through a real period of struggling with my own sense of sexual integrity and purity when . . . INSERT YOUR OWN MINI TESTIMONY HERE.
I felt like I'd really messed up. Can you identify? Did you feel ruined? Let's test those feelings against Scripture for just a second . . .
In Who Moved the Goalpost? *Bob encourages us to get off the roller coaster and to begin to climb the spiral mountain. Let's look at the three spiritual truths of the spiral mountain.* (Display your poster board of the spiral mountain.)

• *Point Number One—I was not born pure. "Surely I was sinful at birth, sinful from the time my mother conceived me" (Psalm 51:5). "There is not a righteous man on earth who does what is right and never sins" (Ecclesiastes 7:20). OK, you weren't born yesterday, so you can handle this: YOU WEREN'T BORN PURE. You were innocent when you were born, but those Scriptures say you were born sinful. So, any notion that you have "lost" your purity is nonsense. You may never have had it.*

I think a lot of time we confuse purity with virginity. As long as we don't cross that virgin line, we're pure. The problem with that is there are a lot of things we can do this side of virginity to sin sexually . . . to rob a lot of the innocence we were born with. Innocence is where you begin, and it is possible that you have lost some of your innocence, but purity . . . that's where you end up! (Point to the top of your spiral mountain.)

• *Point Number Two—In Luke 17:1a Jesus says that things that cause people to sin are bound to come! So, it is a given. I will face the monster of lust in my life. (Draw a scary lust monster across the lowest pathway of your spiral mountain.) It might come in the form of being tempted to use language about girls that's sexual or dishonoring, it might come in the form of being tempted with looking at pornography on the Internet, or it might come in the form of being tempted to give your heart or your body away in a relationship. Temptation is inevitable. It is not a sin in itself . . . this is the exciting part . . . facing that is a chance to pursue purity. Each of us was born with Lust hanging around. The dude is just sitting there waiting for us to get to him. As we choose to journey toward a close relationship with God, he rears his ugly head.*

One of three things will happen when you meet Lust. You'll breeze past him with God's help. Or he'll taunt and tease you pretty effectively . . . maybe causing you to sin . . . but you eventually struggle past him. Or you just get stuck there with him for a long, long, long time.

Hopefully, you're one who makes it past him and says, "Whew! Made it." And you journey on. But suddenly one day, you notice (because you are walking in a spiral) that there he is again. He doesn't look quite as scary because you have seen him before, but you think, No way! I fought with you before. You're a part of the past. *But there he is and you have to go on.*

(INSERT YOUR OWN MINI-TESTIMONY HERE ABOUT A TIME WHEN YOU'VE BEEN TEMPTED AS AN ADULT BUT SAID NO!)

Let's read something together. Turn to page 66 in Who Moved the Goalpost? *Let's read that bold text at the bottom where C. S. Lewis tells us about facing that monster of lust.* (Read or have a good reader read the C. S. Lewis "red lizard" story out loud.)

• *Point Number 3—OK, back to the Spiral. The good news is that each and every evil dude we face on our journey can, like C. S. Lewis's little red lizard, be completely transformed. And as you make right choices, that wimpy little beast turns into something wonderful for God. Purity is the opposite of the sin of lust.* (At the top of the mountain, write "purity" into the flag.) *So, as you confront lust and make right choices with the help of God and friends and lots of fast, strategic exits . . . that little monster, Lust, slowly becomes a contented, uncompromised companion—Purity.*

I felt so relieved when I first had the Spiral explained to me. You see, I felt so guilty for always running into Lust. He was smaller and his roar less threatening each time, but he kept showing up. The fact that he showed up to taunt me, I learned, was not my sin . . . it was a given and a chance to walk deeper into the Spiral and closer to my dear God. Purity is a process. What a freeing secret . . .

- *I was not born pure.*
- *I will face the beast of Lust, perhaps over and over again, but that in itself is not a sin but rather a chance to develop my purity by talking to God, talking to a friend, and making a fast strategic exit.*
- *I can become pure.*

I think it is really important that you grasp this. Understand that you are going to run into this guy Lust most of your life. Be ready for him and know that saying no to him is what pushes you in that direction toward purity.

Understanding that purity is a process is the first strategy in the sexual integrity game plan.

Let's just challenge one another to pursue purity. Look inside yourself right now. If there were a little red lizard on your shoulder, what would he be called . . . ?

- *An unfaithful mind . . . one that fantasizes?*
- *Eyes that are addicted to sexual images?*
- *Too many movies that get your mind wandering from a pure lifestyle?*
- *Maybe God is tugging at your heart to give up a relationship that is not holy?*
- *Maybe you've still not received healing and forgiveness for mistakes in your past?*

Understand that you can BECOME *pure. God desires that* YOU *become pure!*

alone time

Alone Time
Graffiti Wall • 10 Minutes

(Prior to the session, have someone spread out the poster paper; and scatter markers, crayons, and colored pencils across it.)

Play a CD of worship music while you talk and while the guys do this activity. The object is to do this as alone time even though they will be all together on the "graffiti wall." There should be no talking.

I want you to close your eyes and visualize that little red lizard in your life. Everyone has something. All of us, the mentors included, are going to do this with you. What is that red lizard in your life? Now let's all quickly walk over to the brown paper on the floor. I want us to each quietly draw some graffiti there representing the red lizard and how it makes you feel.

(Give the guys five to eight minutes to draw and color.)

Now I would like you to grab that picture you've just drawn and rip it out in the shape of a cross. As you do this, you are acknowledging that the power to overcome this little monster lies in the cross of Jesus. Spend a moment in prayer as you hold that cross in your hands.

Invite the guys to move into their small groups.

small group workshop

Small Group Workshop • 15 Minutes

It is important to really reaffirm to these guys that you are there with them. They are not alone. They need to know they aren't hanging out on a weak limb all by themselves. In this small group session, just talk. Review what they've just learned and ask them what they think. Find ways to encourage them to continue to open up.

Finally, present them each with a Slinky to remind them that the spiral mountain moves them up and closer to God. They may run into some nasty dudes in their journey to become Christlike, but they'll be making progress.

CHOOSING THE RIGHT TEAMMATES

objective:
To begin to strengthen the relationship between the attendees and the mentors and to convince them that they are not alone.

action:
To worship the One who must be the greatest love of their lives—Jesus—and to hear the testimonies of adult men who are currently pursuing purity.

items needed:
A campfire sets a great atmosphere for this session (optional).
If a campfire is not an option, try to get glow sticks to make this fun (optional).
A worship leader

preparation activities:
Read chapters 4, 5, and 15 in *Who Moved the Goalpost?*
Ask the mentors to read chapters 4, 5, and 15 in *Who Moved the Goalpost?*

lesson at a glance

SESSION 3 AT A GLANCE

ACTIVITY	MINUTES	WHAT ATTENDEES DO
Worship Time	*10*	*Worship Jesus through songs familiar to them*
Alone Time	*10*	*Read chapter 4: "I'm All Alone Here"*
Challenge	*40*	*Listen to testimonies of mentors*

worship time

Worship Time
Large Group Worship • 10 Minutes
It is best to have this part of the event in a different, quieter setting. A campfire is a great place for this. If you can't do a campfire, try setting the mood by lowering the lights and using glow sticks to hang around the guys' necks. Something simple like this can set the time apart as special.

To begin with, it would be great to have some time of worship. You may select one of the mentors with musical talent or bring someone in for just this time. It's important to set the tone for this session. It is one of respect and honor. If you don't have a worship leader, consider worshiping to some CDs.

alone time

Alone Time
Read Chapter 4 • 10 Minutes

I'd like to ask you to begin to prepare your hearts. In just a few minutes, several of us will be sharing with you our testimonies about sexual integrity and purity. We're going to be real honest and transparent with you. We need your honor and respect to do this because it's not really that easy. Is it ever easy for guys to talk about their private struggles with sexuality? No, it's not, but it is important to do that. I'd like you to open your copy of Who Moved the Goalpost? *and read chapter 15, which begins on page 157. During this alone time, I'll play worship music for you. When the music changes from quiet, worshipful music to more upbeat, that is your signal to form a circle around me to hear the testimonies of the adults who are here to encourage you.*

large group challenge

Large Group Challenge
Testimonies • 40 Minutes

Each adult present should have about three to five minutes to tell his story about sexual purity. There are two lies you will be destroying when you transparently share. These are exposed in chapters 4 and 5.

The first is the belief many of these young guys have that "I'm all alone here." In sharing, you are saying that they aren't alone. You are in the same boat as you yield to God's plan for your sexual desires.

The second is that "It'll go away when I'm married." If you are married, don't try to say that you don't struggle with sexual temptation if you still do. This only fuels the misconception that these poor guys need only wait until they are married to end this difficult tension between honoring God with their bodies and struggling with lust. Let them know that now is the time to fight the battle, because it doesn't go away without God's help.

Finally, these guys need to hear that sexual integrity is possible. Hopefully, there will be some single men attending who are still virgins or married men who were virgins on their wedding day. Don't discount that. Celebrate it. Don't hide behind other kinds of temptations. Let them know that you are proud of that part of your journey for purity.

After testimonies, conclude the time with a worship song. Invite the guys to pray out loud prayers of thanks to God for these testimonies and the men who have shared them. Encourage them to offer positive feedback to a man if his testimony encouraged them.

THE WORLD'S SEX

objective:
To identify the lies Satan tells us about sex and to begin to develop the ability to intelligently combat them with medical, emotional, and spiritual truth.

action:
To watch "No Apologies," a video by Focus on the Family which features testimonies of men and women with regard to sexual misuse.

items needed:
A large panel (3' x 5' approximately) of tempered glass
Several paint pens or thick permanent markers
"No Apologies" video

preparation activities:
Review the "No Apologies" video.
Read page 23 in *Who Moved the Goalpost?* to begin thinking about STDs.

lesson at a glance

SESSION 4 AT A GLANCE

ACTIVITY	MINUTES	WHAT ATTENDEES DO
Challenge	*15*	*Think about the messages about sex they hear regularly*
Video	*30*	*Watch "No Apologies" (For the video, call 1-800-A-FAMILY.)*
Small Group	*15*	*Discuss what they learned about the opinions about sex*

large group challenge

Large Group Challenge
A Glass Wall of Lies, Part A • 15 Minutes
You will want to do this session outside or in a room where you can make a total mess and not be concerned with damaging property. (At the end of another session, you'll be breaking your "Glass Wall of Lies.") Ahead of the session, set your tempered glass wall in a place where it can stand sturdily and be easily viewed. Using the paint markers (sold in craft stores and departments) or permanent markers, write "I'm all alone here" and "It'll go away when I'm married" in graffiti style on the wall of glass. You'll be inviting the attendees to write any lies they've heard about sex on this panel during this session.

I really want us to focus on the lies that we hear about sex. I think there are a lot of them. In our first session, we talked about two that a lot of guys fall for. One is, "I'm all alone here!" Hopefully, after the testimonies you heard from the mentors you don't believe that anymore. The second is, "It'll go away when I'm married!" As you can see also from these testimonies, a problem with lust is not gotten rid of through natural sexual expression because, oddly enough, they are not the same thing. So it's time to put all the lies out on the table so that we can get rid of them now rather than carry that baggage around all of our lives.

I'm pretty sure these aren't the only two lies you've heard and maybe believed. I'd like to give you the chance to yell out a lie and then come up here and add it to our graffiti wall.

(They should be able to come up with twenty to thirty lies. Let them take time to really think about it, since many lies they've heard so many times don't even sound like lies anymore. They'll say things like "If you love someone it's OK." "Sex can be made safe." "If you don't have sex, you have a hang-up." "Everyone's doing it." "If you don't try it out before marriage, how will you know you're sexually compatible?" And more. Keep emphasizing that these are lies. Say the word *lies* frequently. Read the following example.) *Yes! That's a great lie. But it's just that . . . a lie. Come on up here and add it to our wall. Who else can tell me another lie you hear about sex?*

(After about ten minutes of this, you'll begin to introduce the video.)

Great work on identifying some of those lies. We're going to watch a video now entitled "No Apologies." In it you'll see a lot of teen and single adults talking about sex. See if you can further identify some of the lies they've believed, some of the consequences of believing those lies, and maybe some truth hidden in there.

video

Video
"No Apologies" • 30 Minutes

Play the video. It is strongly recommended that you purchase this video. It is appropriate for middle school through young adult age groups.

small group workshop

Small Group Workshop
Discussion of Video Content • 15 Minutes

You will have briefed the small group mentors to discuss the video. They should ask questions such as "What stuck out to you in that video? What were some of the specific stories that impacted you? What were some of the consequences to premarital sexual activity?"

Let the guys take time to really think about it, because many lies they've heard are things they've heard so many times they don't even sound like lies anymore.

session 5

THE TRUTH ABOUT SEX

objective:

To recognize the covenant purpose of sex as well as the earthly blessings that God rewards us with if that covenant is protected.

action:

To "research" and learn about sex according to God's Word.

items needed:

Four large colorful poster boards or foam corkboards
Colored markers, crayons, and colored pencils
Old magazines
Lots of three-dimensional scraps such as yarn, old keys, coins, pasta, beads, etc.
Glue
Copies of the four different worksheets following this session
A large, heavy tool capable of breaking your glass wall

preparation activities:

Read chapters 7 and 8 in *Who Moved the Goalpost?*
Divide the small groups into four groups even if you have more or fewer than four.
Determine which group will do each small group activity. The options are:

- It's a blood covenant.
- It's a spiritual portrait that enhances intimacy.
- It creates life.
- It's sheer pleasure.

lesson at a glance

SESSION 5 AT A GLANCE		
ACTIVITY	**MINUTES**	**WHAT ATTENDEES DO**
Challenge	*5*	*Hear a brief challenge and receive assignments*
Small Group	*35*	*"Research" one part of God's definition of sex*
Challenge	*20*	*Listen to their peers' interpretation of God's gift of sex*

large group challenge

Large Group Challenge
Introduction • 5 Minutes

(For the beginning of this session, you will need to have your glass wall of lies set up in a place where you can safely shatter the glass. Since this is tempered glass it will separate into thousands of tiny pieces and crash to the ground rather than exploding into large, sharp pieces. However, it is still important to keep a good distance between you, the guys, and the glass so that none of the little pieces can hurt anyone. Hide the large tool you'll be breaking the wall with in your pocket and stand in front of the glass wall with the guys a good twenty feet away.

It's time to break through Satan's wall of lies. They are just that. Lies. They are broken and exposed by truth and that's what we're going to do in this session. We're going to crash through this wall.

(At this point, pull the tool out of your pocket and move away from the wall. A firm, direct hit to the middle of the glass will break it but it must be a hard hit.)

It's not easy to break through these lies and there's one last big one I want to tell you about.

One of Satan's sex lies that we somehow believe is that "Sex is a four-letter word!" Well, at least within the church. We shouldn't really use that word there! Well, sex is not a four-letter word. Sex is an absolutely amazing gift which God is proud to give us.

God loves sex. Just look at Solomon's sexually graphic "song" about his honeymoon. Just before he puts down this pen, he lets us hear the last words uttered on that sensual night when God Himself comes to bless their night of ecstacy. The Lord said, "Eat, O friends, and drink; drink your fill, O lovers" (Song of Songs 5:1). God honors sexuality.

God knew what He was doing when He created women to be utterly tempting. A woman's body is a carefully crafted masterpiece. Sex is the gift God gives us to receive that masterpiece as a part of us. There's no big secret about it, just plain, simple fantastic truth. In this session, I'd like us to uncover that wonderful truth according to God's Word. It's nothing like the sex you and I see portrayed every day in casual, cheap sex scenes on TV, billboards, and at movie theaters.

Rather than having me teach this to you, I'd like to hear you teach each other. There's something very powerful about hearing your friends verbalize God's truth. So, you are now going to move into your small group (or explain how they will be divided so that there are four groups). *You are going to do your own research there, and come back to report to the large group what you have learned about the definition of sex according to God.*

small group workshop

Small Group Workshop
Research Projects • 35 Minutes

Each group has its own different set of instructions. They will basically be digging into and discussing chapters 7 and 8 in *Who Moved the Goalpost?* Each will be assigned to one portion of the definition. For each of the four groups, provide the appropriate copy of one of the following four worksheets, which takes them through their assignment. Once they have completed their worksheets, they'll be making a creative poster board to demonstrate what they've learned and to teach the key truths to the rest of the large group.

Large Group Challenge
Peer Teaching • 20 Minutes
Beginning with "It's a blood covenant," let each group take two to three minutes to briefly share what they learned. Be sure to read the chapters thoroughly and fill in any key thoughts or verses they have left out so that the entire group understands the concept. Give the first group a full five minutes, as they have the most information to share. Give the others two to three minutes.

At the end of this session, thank God for teaching you during this time. Ask the attendees to utter one-sentence prayers of thanks to God for the gift of sexuality and the specific things they learned.

WORKSHEET FOR GROUP NUMBER ONE

IT'S A BLOOD COVENANT

Yours is the most important of the four purposes of sex. Dig deeply and be prepared to explain this wonderful spiritual truth to the rest of the group just thirty-five minutes from now. For the sake of time, you may want to break your group into two in order to complete both tasks. Be sure to allow yourself some time to talk about what you've discovered and to create a poster at the end.

1. Assign each of the verses to one or two members of your group to read aloud.
   Proverbs 2:17
   Romans 12:1–2
   Matthew 25:1–13
   Ephesians 5:31–32

   What does Proverbs 2:17 call marriage?
   What does Romans 12:1–2 beg us to consider our bodies to be?
   As Jesus talks about the ten virgins, what is He really explaining?
   What great spiritual "mystery" does Ephesians 5:31–32 say the sexual union represents?

2. Read chapter 7 in *Who Moved the Goalpost?* Be prepared to summarize what you learned to your small group and to the large group. You may choose to read any parts of the chapter that are significant to you.

   What three characteristics mark a biblically defined covenant? (pages 72–74)
   How do we see these characteristics in the gift of sex? (pages 74–75)
   What is portrayed through marriage according to Jewish customs? (pages 76–77)

3. As a team, make a poster that creatively displays what you've learned. You may decorate your poster in any manner you'd like. You will be using this to present your truths to the large group in just a few minutes. Work quickly, but don't miss any of this very important material.

4. Assign two guys in your group to present the key truths. They may want to review and prepare while the rest of you work on the poster. Your group will have five minutes or less to present.

WORKSHEET FOR GROUP NUMBER TWO

IT'S A SPIRITUAL PORTRAIT THAT ENHANCES INTIMACY

If we experience sex as God intended, it is blessed in three ways. This particular truth is a concept that's kind of hard for guys to wrap their brains around. Your task is to find a way to make the rest of the large group grasp this great spiritual truth!

1. Assign each of the verses to one or two members of your group to read aloud.
   Genesis 2:24
   Ephesians 5:31–,32

   What does Genesis say we become when we are married?
   What word does Ephesians use to describe the level of intimacy a marriage should have?

2. Read chapter 8, pages 82–84 in *Who Moved the Goalpost?* Be prepared to summarize what you learned to your small group and to the large group. You may choose to read any parts of the chapter that are significant to you.

   What did the youth pastor at Bob's church, Jonathan Weibel, have to say about spiritual intimacy and marriage? (page 82)
   What did Eve's presence do for Adam? (page 83)
   What did a survey of the prayer lives of married couples display? (page 84)

3. As a team, make a poster that creatively displays what you've learned. You may decorate your poster in any manner you'd like. You will be using this to present your truths to the large group in just a few minutes. Work quickly, but don't miss any of this very important material.

4. Assign two guys in your group to present the key truths. They may want to review and prepare while the rest of you work on the poster. Your group will have only three minutes or less to present. Be prepared!

WORKSHEET FOR GROUP NUMBER THREE

IT CREATES LIFE

If we experience sex as God intended, it is blessed in three ways. This truth may seem pretty simple, but . . . think about it . . . it's so very complex. Try to find that as you prepare to explain this truth to the large group in just a short while.

1. Assign the key verse to a member of your group to read aloud.
Genesis 1:28a

What does God command us to do in this verse?
So, what purpose does the act of marriage fulfill?

2. Read page 85 in *Who Moved the Goalpost?* Be prepared to summarize what you learned to your small group and to the large group. You may choose to read any parts of the chapter that are significant to you.

How does Bob describe his emotions during his wife's first pregnancy?
What do you think about the fact that God creates a life from two tiny microscopic cells?
What does it feel like to think about seeing a life that reflects yours? Your eyes, maybe, or your "walk" or your hair?
How do you think creating life before you were married would compare with the experience after you were married?

3. As a team, make a poster that creatively displays what you've learned. You may decorate your poster in any manner you'd like. You will be using this to present your truths to the large group in just a few minutes. Work quickly, but don't miss any of this very important material.

4. Assign two guys in your group to present the key truths. They may want to review and prepare while the rest of you work on the poster. Your group will have less than three minutes to present.

WORKSHEET FOR GROUP NUMBER FOUR

IT'S SHEER PLEASURE

If we experience sex as God intended, it is blessed in three ways. It's probably not going to be too difficult to have the other guys grasp the concept you're presenting. After all, today's culture reminds us daily that sex is fun, but I want you to look at this really closely. I think you'll discover something new!

1. Assign the key verse to a member of your group to read aloud.
Proverbs 5:18–19

Are you surprised that this verse is in God's Word?
What part of it tells you that one of God's purposes for sex is fun?

2. Read pages 86–88 in *Who Moved the Goalpost?* Be prepared to summarize what you learned to your small group and to the large group. You may choose to read any parts of the chapter that are significant to you.

Going back to Proverbs 5:18,19, what new twist does the Hebrew definition offer to your understanding of this verse? (page 86)
What does the study entitled "Sex in America" do to your understanding of Scripture and God's plan for sexuality? (page 87)
What effect can playing around sexually without actually having sexual intercourse have upon a marriage? (pages 87–88)

3. As a team, make a poster that creatively displays what you've learned. You may decorate your poster in any manner you'd like. You will be using this to present your truths to the large group in just a few minutes. Work quickly, but don't miss any of this very important material.

4. Assign two guys in your group to present the key truths. They may want to review and prepare while the rest of you work on the poster. Your group will have less than three minutes to present.

ENTICEMENT

objective:
To learn to recognize enticement-passive temptation in their lives.

action:
To identify areas in their own lives where the risk is apparent.

items needed:
A large glass bottle or pickle jar with a fake brain in it or a large photo of a brain
A sign reading "A Guy's Primary Sexual Organ: Please Do Not Touch!"
A cloth large enough to cover your "brain display"
A poster board or dry erase board with the graphic brainteaser drawn on it
Chocolate bars
A hunting snare
Materials to make mini-snares
Photocopies of handouts provided after this session

preparation activities:
Read chapter 9 in *Who Moved the Goalpost?*
Practice making mini-snares.

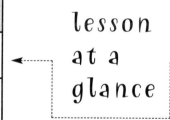

SESSION 6 AT A GLANCE		
ACTIVITY	**MINUTES**	**WHAT ATTENDEES DO**
Challenge	*30*	*Be challenged to maintain their brains!*
Small Group	*30*	*Identify areas where the snares have been set and enticement is possible*

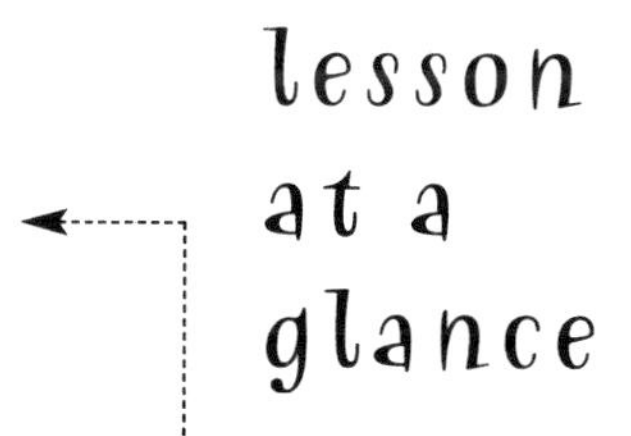

Large Group Challenge
Maintain Your Brain • 15 Minutes

Prior to the session, you will have placed your brain in a jar or your picture of a brain under the fabric and have "A Guy's Primary Sexual Organ" sign displayed in front of it. Don't say anything about this. Just give them time to wonder and imagine, even though they may imagine the wrong thing! You'll soon be making a memorable statement for them.

I have a few brainteasers to wake you up. Get in your small groups in small clusters around the room. I'm going to offer you several brainteasers to solve. The first small group to send me a representative with the correct answer gets chocolate bars for the entire group. (Give them time to get into their groups and then read each brainteaser. You may read the longer ones more than once if needed. Give them as much time as needed to solve it without your help.)

Brainteaser: What has a bark but makes no sound?
Solution: A tree

Brainteaser: Who is the murderer? Crime: A wealthy woman was murdered with a knife in her bedroom at 12:00 noon, May 26, 1986, in Rye, New York. Suspects and Alibis: Husband: In library reading. Gardener: Playing gin rummy with wife. Butler: At bank cashing paycheck. Cook: In kitchen baking apple pie.
Solution: Butler (Memorial Day—banks are closed.)

Brainteaser: What familiar phrase or cliché is this?
(This is a graphic brainteaser. You'll have to display the following picture for the guys to see.)

TIDE

Solution: High tide

Brainteaser: Solve the following:
- *Twin girls became separated at age 1.*
- *They are reunited 18 years later.*
- *The twins discover they were born in different years.*
- *Further investigation uncovered records verifying this information.*

How is this possible?
Solution: One was born December 31, just before midnight. The other was born minutes later, just after midnight.

Brainteaser: Tom's father is now twice his son's age. Ten years ago he was three times his age. How old is Tom's father?

Solution: Forty years old

(These brainteasers come from a game named "Nogginnosh," which is an excellent resource for all youth groups and families. It contains over 1,000 brainteasers, many of which are visual and require you to have the game cards. To order it call 503-284-1114.)

Great work, teams! Now, I have one final brainteaser for you.
Brainteaser: What is a guy's primary sexual organ?
Solution: (Don't tell them. Give them clues such as . . . "You all just used it!" or "It's higher than you might think." They may get it. When they do, unveil the fake brain as you announce the answer!) *The brain is a guy's primary sexual organ.*

It's simple science! Our sexual organs are activated by the body's autonomic nervous system (ANS). This system—headquartered in the brain—is not controlled by the will but by the environment. For example, let's imagine you are sixteen. (Maybe you are!) Let's imagine your dad told you not to drive the car, but you did and . . . uh-oh . . . you had a fender bender. As you sit there sweating about it, and you suddenly hear him coming home for the day, your body would physically respond. You might experience a rapid pulse, sweat, and perhaps even heavy breathing. You might get a sick feeling in your stomach. You cannot control these things by choice. You are scared out of your wits and your body is telling you about it! Now, how you act when Dad comes around the corner—take a quick hike up to the bedroom to hide or stand firm to tell the truth—is entirely up to you. But your body's initial response was not controlled by your will but by the environment.

Sexual arousal works the same way in guys. Things in the environment—what we see, what we hear, and what we smell—work together to tell the brain that the time is right for sexual arousal. At that time, the brain sends chemicals through your body. Your pulse changes, you experience a change in body temperature, and your penis begins to become erect. You have been aroused! You may not have willfully created these reactions in your body, but the environment created them.

Just like in our car-wreck scenario, when you had a choice with what you did with the fear when Dad came home, you have a choice with what you will do when you initially become sexually aroused. (But don't rely on it. An aroused guy doesn't have much of a conscience sometimes.) You can get outta there or think about something to diminish the response. But it's way too easy to let your imagination run with it as you fantasize about what could come next.

Here's a quick test for you. Have you ever:

- *Gone to an R-rated movie that had a sex scene?*
- *Laughed at the sexual innuendos on one of the most popular TV shows?*
- *Glanced through a magazine filled with sexually charged advertising?*

- *Stumbled onto an Internet porn site?*

If you answered "yes" to any (or all) of these, I have news for you. You've compromised your mental virginity. That may sound harsh, but I believe it's true. It's kind of like this hunter's snare here. (Show them the hunter's snare.)

This isn't your typical steel foothold trap, which looks painful and nasty with its iron teeth. When an animal steps into one of those, the springs respond and trap the animal in the iron teeth of the trap. The animal knows immediately that it's been caught. Some animals will even chew off their legs to get away from the torture. The capture is apparent. The springs are what empower it.

This snare is different. This is a piece of simple steel cable. It forms a loop. It looks pretty nonthreatening. Why don't one of you act as my animal? Go ahead and walk through that snare as if you were a deer or a bear, and act just like you think they would. (The person should walk through it and try to run from it when he feels tension. An animal would not be calm. If the volunteer didn't do this, have fun letting another guy try.) *An animal usually walks calmly through a snare. It just keeps walking through it until it feels tension, when it begins to pull harder and press ever forward. It doesn't realize that if it had backed out early, it could have gotten away. When it recognizes it is stuck, it's too late. The capture is subtle. It is empowered by the animal's own actions.*

That's kind of how we lose our mental virginity. It's not obvious that we're being trapped by lust. It's subtle. Our own choices to move forward and push the envelope on what we see are actually empowering lust and exposing us mentally to sexual perversion. We think it's OK, because everyone else is headed in the same direction, but it's not OK. Ephesians 4:17–19 of The Message *Bible reads: "[Let] there be no going along with the crowd, the empty-headed, mindless crowd. They've refused for so long to deal with God that they've lost touch not only with God but with reality itself. They can't think straight anymore. Feeling no pain, they let themselves go in sexual obsession, addicted to every sort of perversion."*

Doesn't that sound like the snare? They "feel no pain" so they let themselves go.

Now, let's not be too unreasonable here. Today it's nearly impossible to completely avoid all of the temptation you'll find on billboards, girls who aren't wearing much, and just plain fantastic-looking girls. This is enticement. Enticement is passive temptation. You didn't realize you were going to run into temptation. You passively walked into it.

But be warned. Enticement can be a lot like that snare. Exposing yourself to it—whether you're surfing the net unfiltered or just watching sexually charged comedy with some friends—is like walking through the snare. It's harder to be overcome by enticement when you establish boundaries to avoid it.

You're going to move into your small groups and have an honest talk about what kinds of enticement you've been facing.

Sexual Integrity Challenge

Maintain Your Brain!

Are you protecting your mental virginity? Or have you been trapped? Worse yet, have you been giving in to the slow control of snarelike enticements? Put a check mark by the appropriate column.

	Maintaining My Brain!	I'm Entering the Snare!	I've Been Trapped!
In the movies I see?			
In the television I watch?			
In the parties I go to?			
In the clothes I wear?			
In the way I use the Internet?			
In the way I talk about girls?			
In the way my friends talk about girls?			
In the places I go with girls?			
In the things I do with girls on dates?			

Overall I:

_____ Am doing well. I m not corrupting my mental virginity as a common practice.

_____ Am waaaay too close to it all, and I need to establish some new guidelines.

_____ Am trapped. Help! I need to make some changes.

small group challenge

Small Group Challenge
Snare Worksheet • 30 Minutes

In small groups, each mentor will pass out the "Sexual Integrity Challenge" entitled "Maintain Your Brain!" Give each guy a few minutes to fill his out, and then discuss them. In what areas are they maintaining their brains, empowering the snares, or trapped? Do they see the danger of enticements? Based on their own evaluations, what do they need to do to maintain their brains?

Ask them to turn to page 99 in their copy of *Who Moved the Goalpost?* Read aloud the "Autobiography in Five Short Chapters." Ask them how this story applies to their lives.

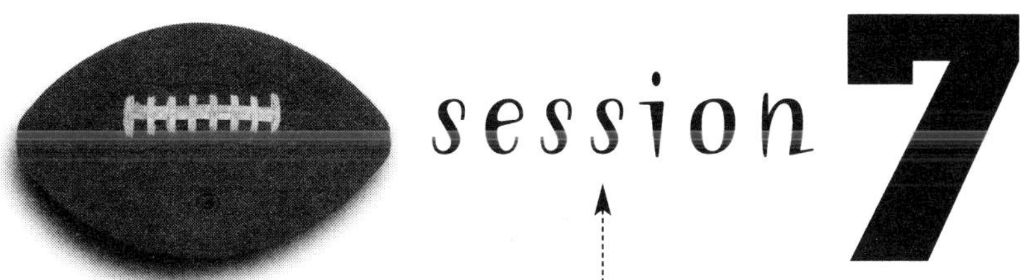

objective:

To recognize the presence of muscle memory triggers—repeated, expected temptations in their lives—and to learn how to avoid them.

MUSCLE MEMORY TRIGGERS

action:

To identify specific times, events, and mediums which are muscle memory triggers.

items needed:

- *Jaws* soundtrack

Each small group will need the following items that will not be usable ever again:

- One empty two-liter soda bottle
- One old VCR tape
- One old scratched or broken CD
- One contemporary magazine that today's mainstream guys might read

preparation activities:

Read chapter 10 in *Who Moved the Goalpost?*

lesson at a glance

SESSION 7 AT A GLANCE		
ACTIVITY	**MINUTES**	**WHAT ATTENDEES DO**
Game Time	*5*	*Play Media Mash*
Challenge	*10*	*Learn what muscle memory triggers are*
Alone Time	*25*	*Identify muscle memory triggers*
Small Group	*20*	*Ask their buddies to hold them accountable*

game time

Game Time

Media Mash • 5 Minutes

Media Mash is a game that teaches us to be mindful of what we put into our minds. Tell the guys that they have three minutes to get the VCR, CD, and magazine into their soda bottle. Tell them the winning team is the one with all of their media in the bottle with the bottle still intact. Then start the clock. No further explanation is needed. Some will immediately start destroying their media mix to get it into the mouth of the bottle. Others will soon follow suit.

As the teams finish, cheer and shout!
When they've all finished, ask: *Can you get it out now?*

large group challenge

Large Group Challenge • 15 Minutes

That's the big question. Once all that media is in there, can you get it out? Let's take a simple sound test. Let's say I'm going to play some superbly written orchestra music. What would you expect? (Let them answer. Most will say "sleeper" music or "boring.") *OK, close your eyes and listen.* (Play the *Jaws* theme song.) *Unsettling, isn't it! Those are the same instruments that play our "Star Spangled Banner," but when they play the* Jaws *theme, they stir up fearful visuals and unsettling emotions. Why?* (Let them respond, eventually getting to the fact that people were trained to fear that sound by the movie that accompanied it.) *Our brains are programmable. What we get in there is hard to get out. So, if you watch enough sexually explicit movies, you'll begin to be programmed to think sexually. I want you to take a look at this in some quiet time we're going to give you right now. During this time you will read chapter 10 in* Who Moved the Goalpost? *and you will do the exercise on the last page of it. You have twenty-five minutes to work quietly in this room and then we'll gather into our small groups.*

alone time

Alone Time • 25 Minutes

During this time, the guys will be reading chapter 10 in *Who Moved the Goalpost?*. They will also be doing the writing assignment on page 110 in this chapter. If the mentors take this time seriously, so will the guys. The adults can a) do the same thing they are doing or b) walk around the room or sit in the room while they pray for the guys.

small group challenge

Small Group Challenge • 20 Minutes

Small groups leaders should begin. As a leader you should share very briefly what patterns you've identified in your own life and how you will avoid your triggers. Then tell the guys that you'd like to hear their triggers so you can hold them accountable and so that their buddies can also hold them accountable. Let them share as they feel comfortable. If they don't, you can probe with questions like: "How many of you found that watching TV late at night is a trigger?" or "Any of you find that surfing the net is a trigger to sexual sin?" or "Did anyone identify a time of the day when they are most tempted?"

When all of the guys have had time to share and you are coming to a close on your time, ask them to pray in groups of two or three for each other.

GUARDING HER FUTURE

objective:
To establish boundaries within dating relationships, recognizing the great emotional damage sexual misuse can cause to a girl.

items needed:
Each small group will need the following items:

- One raw egg (have a few extras on hand in case of early mishaps.)
- Ten plastic drinking straws
- Two feet of masking tape
- One standard-sized ladder
- A large plastic tarp for under the ladder (or you can do this outside)

preparation activities:
Read chapters 11 and 12 in *Who Moved the Goalpost?*

Invite two to three women to share their testimonies of sexual purity. Your selection has to be prayerfully considered. This is a powerful opportunity. These need to be women who are in their late twenties or older. They need to have testimonies they can share in which tremendous healing from dating baggage and perhaps sexual sin occurred. They need to be extremely mature so that they can candidly share the great heartache that their sexual sin and wreckless dating created without completely "male bashing" or blaming all of the sin on the guy. The guys won't relate to a girl who was intentionally trashed by a guy. They won't see themselves in that. They may relate to a girl who talks about a dating relationship where her heart got tangled up and things got heated up and ended badly. These women will have two to five minutes to briefly share their stories which need to have ended in God's healing and perhaps even dating and marrying the right way . . . with a guy who demonstrated protective qualities and honor for her.

lesson at a glance

SESSION 8 AT A GLANCE		
ACTIVITY	**MINUTES**	**WHAT ATTENDEES DO**
Game Time	*20*	*Certified Egg Protection Device*
Challenge	*30*	*Take the Relationship Rookie/NFL All-Star Test*
Small Group	*10*	*Establish boundaries for dating situations*

game time

Game Time
Certified Egg Protection Device • 20 Minutes

Ahead of time, set the ladder up in the area where you will conduct this session. When it's time to begin, issue one raw egg, ten plastic drinking straws, and two feet of masking tape to each small group. Inform them that the U.S. Dairy Association has need of a new patented Certified Egg Protection Device. Funding is low, so the only materials for this device are ten plastic egg protection tubes (straws) and two feet of standard stickage line (tape). This device must past the rigorous test of the egg being dropped from the top of the egg protection device challenger (ladder). Your team has eight minutes to develop your prototype prior to testing. The winning team will receive a life's supply of eggs or a treasure chest of products containing egg ingredients (a shoe box filled with chocolate bars. The incentive is necessary. Trust me. Guys actually like to see things self-destruct. The chocolate bars are your insurance that they'll give this thing a try!) Start your timer and give the guys eight minutes before you begin "testing."

For testing, ask each group to send you one representative who will drop their Certified Egg Protection Device from the top of the ladder. The team whose egg either does not break or oozes the very least will win. Have a "drop-off" if there is a tie.

large group challenge

Large Group Challenge
Relationship Rookie/NFL/All-Star Test • 30 Minutes

As you can imagine, we did this exercise for a reason. Although this was really crazy and fun, I have a tough truth to share. I want you to be serious about this, so I need you to get comfortable and make a 180° shift in your mentality. (Hey, if I were you, I'd give them a moment to know that you are serious.)

Guys, some of you treat girls with about as much compassion and sincerity as you did those eggs. Some of you do it knowingly. A lot of you do it without even knowing it. But I want you to know that God created those girls to be emotionally fragile. Just as that egg is fragile, the girls you interact with are extremely fragile emotionally. The things you do to them or with them emotionally, physically, and mentally are things that may stay with them all of their lives. The effect can last a lifetime. Some girls may never share the fact that you had sex with them or touched them or enjoyed oral sex with them. They'll even perhaps enjoy the moment, but what they ultimately craved from you is commitment, love, loyalty. In fact, in most cases, what motivates a girl to be sexual with a guy is the fact that her heart has been captured. When they don't find your commitment and loyalty behind a guy's physically driven desires, they are crushed. So crushed, in fact, that the suicide rate among sexually active girls is six times higher than that of her virgin peers. We're talking serious ramifications here, guys, and sometimes it takes a long time to heal.

I've invited a few women from our church to share with you how their own dating years deeply impacted their lives. I'd like you to listen to their hearts.

(Give each woman three to five minutes and thank them and invite them to leave when they've finished. It is a good idea to ask one of the other adult male mentors to escort them out for the express purpose of affirming them. For women it can be very difficult to share such things and not feel vulnerable. Affirm that what they shared was appropriate and needed.)

With those testimonies in your heads, I'd like you to turn to page 113 in your copy of Who Moved the Goalpost? *We're going to read the passage from Galatians highlighted in green at the top of the page.*

(You can select a guy to read it or read it yourself. Read the entire passage out loud.)

This is really a test for us, given by God to evaluate a man's sexual perversion or sexual integrity and strength in dating relationships. I'd like you to turn to page 117 and actually take the test.

(Turn to page 117.)

You have two categories here, based on the Galatians passage. I want you to honestly evaluate yourself, circling the statement that best describes you for each number. You're either Relationship Rookie or an NFL All-Star. Take the test and see.

(Give the guys three to five minutes to take the test.)

As you complete the test, please move into your small groups for some further discussion.

Small Group Sexual Integrity Challenge • 10 Minutes

Small group mentors should read page 132 under "Sexual Integrity Challenge" ahead of time to prepare. They will guide their small group through this exercise, discussing it as they go.

small group challenge

THE ULTIMATE COMPETITION: SHAME VS. GRACE

objective:

To recognize that God's grace is what empowers us to say no to worldly passions and that it's freely extended regardless of the shame the past may bring.

items needed:

Each guy needs a mini Etch-a-Sketch which he'll take home as a souvenir
One large Etch-a-Sketch
One poster board or dry-erase board

preparation activities:

Read chapters 13 and 14 in *Who Moved the Goalpost?*
Make your poster or dry-erase board read "Shame vs. Guilt."
Create a piece of paper that will fit over the word *guilt* which reads "Grace."

SESSION 9 AT A GLANCE		
ACTIVITY	**MINUTES**	**WHAT ATTENDEES DO**
Challenge	*30*	*Visually walk to their most vile moment and receive God's grace*
Alone Time	*15*	*Write a letter to God*
Challenge	*15*	*Pray with their mentors/receive an embrace*

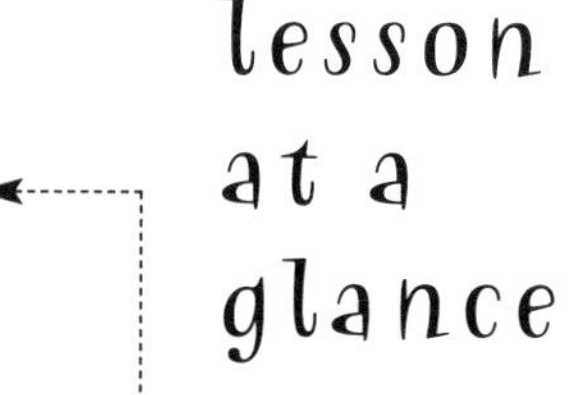

large group challenge

Large Group Challenge • 30 Minutes

Having read the opening narrative in chapter 13, you are going to re-create that experience for the guys. It's important that they understand that this is a serious session, and you expect an attitude of reverence for the truth of God.

> *I'd like you to stretch out on the floor and close your eyes. I'm going to ask you to re-create an experience in your mind. Give yourself lots of room so that you are in your own private space.* (Give them time to stretch out.)
>
> *I'd like you to re-create a scene in your mind, if you will. Only you can do this because you've already been there. I'd like you to imagine back to the vilest thing you've ever done.* (No further description is necessary. Each of us has our own moment of shame that stands heads above the rest. Just give them a few moments to go to the place.)

I want you to picture yourself there at that moment as if you were experiencing it right now. Think about how you feel. See what you are doing. Note the environment around you. (Give them a moment to consider these things.)

Now, I want you to watch as Jesus enters the scene and sees you there. What does Jesus do? (Give them time to think about this.)

OK, I'd like you to open your eyes. There's an Etch-a-Sketch next to you. (These could be quietly laid out while their eyes were closed.) *Using that Etch-a-Sketch, I'd like you to draw what that vile moment feels like to you. Be imaginative and create a contemporary work of art that relates to that moment.* (Give them time to complete the task.)

Now, gently lay your Etch-a-Sketch on the floor in front of you. I'd like to talk to you about that picture.

Without telling me what your picture is about, how does it make you feel? (Invite responses, but be prepared to probe if they do not respond. Let them keep offering answers until someone says the word *shame* or you offer it.) *Shame? How many of you have felt shame? Shame is the last stage of sexual sin. It's the feeling that we get hours after we've acted out in some way. You find yourself with the same lonely, desperate feeling you had the last time you acted out. This is shame.*

Shame is not the same as guilt. (Show the poster board which says "Shame vs. Guilt.") *Guilt can actually benefit us. Guilt is God's tool to address specific sinful behaviors. It tells us we need to redirect our habits and choices. Guilt says, "I should not have done that.* That *was bad." Guilt is like the skin of your soul. It protects your mind and emotions. If your skin touched something that could burn you, it would send impulses to your brain that would help you get out of danger. That's how guilt works.*

Shame, on the other hand, is a tool of Satan which distorts guilt. Shames says, "I am bad." It is a terrible, painful feeling that never ceases. It drives us into a lonelier place where we cannot find accountability or guidance to heal. Shame is like having the skin of your soul ripped off, actually taking with it the emotions that lie beneath.

The Prodigal Son is a good example of a guy who felt some intense shame. The Bible doesn't really say that he was sexually crazed, but the description of him in Luke 15 definitely would place him under the Relationship Rookie category. Take a look at Luke 15. (Give them time to turn in their Bibles or you may read to them.) *How does this guy demonstrate himself to be a Relationship Rookie?*

(Possible answers: He clearly tried to get his own way. His relationship with his dad was about what he could get out of it. He was competitive to the max with his brother. He had small-minded, lopsided pursuits . . . crazy parties night after night to the point of not keeping a job. He was incapable of loving or being loved. He was possibly getting his share of repetitive, loveless sex, but whatever kinds of relationships he did have, they ended badly.)

At the end of the rope, he feels . . . SHAME! He plans to go to his father and say he's "not worthy." Notice he's not saying he made some bad decisions and he regrets the sin in his life. He feels bad about himself. *That's shame.*

What does the father, representative of God, do?

(Possible answers: He runs toward the stench. He embraces the son with his dirty rags and pig-slopped skin. He wraps him in robes of honor.)

The son is greeted, pig slop and waste covered, with warm embraces, loving kisses, and a new, clean robe of honor. He reaches past the sin and extends grace. That, my friend, is what God does. That's what Jesus would do if He found you encrusted in your sin. He would extend to you His grace! (Cover the word *guilt* with *grace*.) *Philip Yancey writes, "Grace means there is nothing we can ever do to make God love us less. There is nothing we can ever do to make God love us more."*

How about now? What do you think God would do if He found you in that vile place you were thinking of moments ago? I think I know. I think He'd run to you. I think He'd embrace you and search for that special new spiritual garment of honor to place on you. But first you have to come to Him, empty-handed, clinging to nothing. Come to Him.

(Pick up your Etch-a-Sketch where you drew your vile moment.) *I'm so glad that this moment that's embedded in my mind is in God's hands, because His grace did this to it.* (Shake the Etch-a-Sketch and erase the lines.) *And His grace will do that to you, if you come to Him.*

We're going to have some alone time here to write a letter to God. In it, I want you to come to Him fresh and repentant. I want you to reach out for God's grace. Give Him that vile moment and any others you need to get rid of. Come to the Savior.

alone time

Alone Time • 15 minutes
Give the guys fifteen minutes to write a letter to God.

Large Group Challenge

If you wrote a letter and truly are turning your back on the sin and returning to Jesus, I want you to just shake that Etch-a-Sketch as you symbolically embrace God's grace. I'm going to invite the mentors to come up here with me. We're here to embrace you just like the father embraced the Prodigal Son and just like Jesus wants to embrace you. If you come up here, we'd like to embrace you and pray for you. (Give them time to come and be prayed for.)

large group challenge

session 10

objective:
To encourage attendees to "develop your dad"

action:
To write a letter to their dad

items needed:
Paper to write letters to their dads

preparation activities:
Read chapters 16 in "Who Moved the Goalpost?"

DEVELOP YOUR DAD

lesson at a glance

SESSION 10 AT A GLANCE		
ACTIVITY	**MINUTES**	**WHAT ATTENDEES DO**
Game Time	*10*	*Play "Believe It Or Not!"*
Challenge	*15*	*Hear how powerful their dad's sexual integrity will be in predicting their own level of success*
Alone Time	*15*	*Write a letter to their dads*
Open Mike	*20*	*Share their own testimonies and commitments*

in this session, you will be seeking to convince the guys that they really must invite their parents into their lives specifically in the area of sexual integrity if they are going to be successful.

game time

Game Time • 10 Minutes
Challenge the guys to break off into groups of two or three. Within those groups, they should share the strangest fact about themselves. Examples of things that have been shared in the past: "I once drove in a drag race," "I've been attacked by a shark and have the scars to prove it." or "I have double-jointed shoulders and can contort my body." If a pair or trio thinks they may have a truly weird fact, bring them to the front. Choose three to five groups to come to the front. Have

each group share their "Believe it or not" weird fact and ask the group to "vote" by cheering for the weirdest. You can give the winner a chocolate bar and a loud standing O!

Large Group Challenge • 5 Minutes

large group challenge

There's just one really important thing left to say. Believe it or not . . . your dad struggles or has struggled with sexual temptation, too.

It's not rocket science. He's in the same boat with you. He's also really important in a way you might not even imagine. You see, we really tend to repeat the things our dad did in this area.

Whether you live in the lap of luxury or in the ghetto, you are guaranteed to inherit some things from your family. Some of them will be great blessings. (Tell them two great things you inherited from your dad; maybe his great hair or sense of humor.)

Some of the things you inherit will not be as welcomed. Exodus 20:5 says that the sins of our fathers are passed on to the children "to the third and fourth generation." Psychologists from all walks of faith agree that we humans tend to inherit the sins of our fathers (and mothers). From the homes of hot tempers come more hot tempers. From the homes of selfish people come more selfish people. From the homes of alcoholics come alcoholics. The prognosis is frightening for some of us.

(Here it is best if you can interject your own testimony of how your dad has positively or negatively affected your quest for sexual integrity. If you are uncomfortable with this, you can use my testimony on pages 169 and 170. Begin with *"I'd known from an early age . . . "* end with *" . . . God's intended plan for my life."*)

The chance is really good that you and your dad can actually start fostering a relationship that can help you . . . and maybe him, too. I'd like to ask you to step out with me and reach out for that. We're going to do it with a simple letter. I want you to write a letter to your dad. Tell him how hard this battle is and that you could use an older and wiser warrior standing beside you. I want you to be raw and real with your dad in this letter. Write it whether you feel you'll be able to give it to him or not. Just write your immediate thoughts. When you've finished, pray over it. Ask God to give you wisdom and courage to share it with your dad. And remember, your mentor this weekend is here to help you with that in whatever way you need support.

Alone Time • 15 Minutes

alone time

(Pass out paper for letters and instruct the guys to respect this time with quiet.) Give them fifteen minutes to write and pray.

open mike time/ challenge

Open Mike Time/Challenge • 20 Minutes

It's time to step up to the plate, guys. You can come to this and just have fun or you can leave here and it can change your life. It's your choice. I have a somewhat silly way to show you what comes next.

Give each guy a potato and one straw. Ask him to push the straw the whole way through the potato. (It CAN be done, if you follow through with the movement and don't stop. A swift continuous motion will do it. Practice in advance so that you can demonstrate.) Though this is a short object lesson, it drives home a vital point! They must follow through with what they have learned. Encourage them to finish reading the book or to start journaling consistently or to invite a man to mentor them or to do whatever God puts on their hearts. Give them a few minutes to reflect on what they need to do to follow through with this retreat. Finish the retreat or ten-week study with an open testimony time. Ask guys to share the biggest thing they learned or to make a public commitment. Encourage boldness as they seek to experience PURE FREEDOM!

Who Moved the Goalpost?

THE TEAM HUDDLE

A Word from Bob Gresh

As the father of a preteen boy, I'm concerned about the struggle with lust that Christian men are facing. Approximately 64 percent of Christian men struggle with sexual addiction or compulsion, which might include pornography, compulsive masturbation, or other secret sexual activities.

That's the information we have on adult men. Though I have yet to find a comprehensive survey on teen guys and sexual compulsions, most of the adults say it started during their teen years. It just never went away. At one Promise Keepers event, half of the men present said they'd viewed pornography in the week preceding the event. Lust is deeply affecting our church, and the problem is growing at a rapid rate. If we want to fight the effects of lust, we've got to start where it begins to take root—during the teen years.

Who Moved the Goalpost? The Team Huddle is an aggressive approach to helping guys before the seduction of this world overtakes them. The event's primary purpose is to give young men practical tools to live a life of purity. Our objectives are simple but powerful. The young men who attend will:

- *Recognize that "you are not alone" in your struggle against lust.*
- *Learn that the issue of sexual purity is a lifelong journey and it won't "go away when I'm married."*
- *Identify the difference between being innocent and being pure.*
- *Establish informal mentorships with men who participate as groups leaders.*
- *Recognize the covenant purpose of sex as well as the earthly blessings that God rewards us with, if that covenant is protected.*
- *Establish boundaries to avoid enticement and muscle memory triggers that arouse desires to masturbate, view pornography, or act out sexually.*
- *Establish specific boundaries to avoid sexual contact with young women.*
- *Witness the emotional turmoil girls face for what may be a lifetime when exposed to sexual sin.*
- *Learn the difference between shame and guilt, and begin to embrace God's grace.*

Oh, and just in case your teen guy is like me and doesn't like boring, speaking-intensive events . . . you can assure him that this one will be high-contact and fun. My educational philosophy is that the most effective kind of learning is experiential. The least effective kind of learning comes from verbal teaching. I believe in active learning. (And I fall asleep when I'm not learning that way!) Everything we do at this event has the intended purpose of teaching . . . even playing Maul Ball! (If only all learning were this fun!)

I hope you'll encourage your son to be there. And, hey, watch out for that goalpost!

Bob

Who Moved the Goalpost?
Is A Pure Freedom Program

Who Moved the Goalpost?

THE TEAM HUDDLE

On the playing field of sexual integrity . . .

Which Guy Are You?

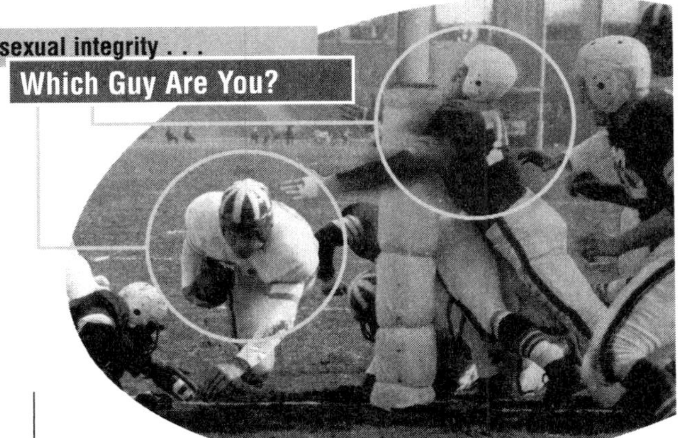

"Powerful advice!"
—Michael Ross, nationally recognized editor

"Lust is the #1 challenge facing Christian men . . . Bob reveals practical strategies to help in the war . . ."
—Clay Crosse, singer/songwriter

"There's nothing like this out there."
—Tony, 19 years old

Pure FREEDOM

Who Moved the Goalpost?
Is A Pure Freedom Program

Until 1974, the NFL's field goalpost was right on the goal line instead of at the back of the end zone as it is today. Sometimes when we're rushing around on the playing field of life, the temptation distracts us and . . . bammmm . . . you're nose deep in the goalpost of lust.

Can you identify?

There is hope. Who Moved the Goalpost? The Team Huddle is a high-contact event that'll revolutionize your view of sexual integrity. Bob Gresh will teach you seven winning strategies in the sexual integrity game plan. And would you believe he'll do it doing crazy stuff like playing Maul Ball?! In the heat of the games, you'll discover answers to vital questions such as:

- Am I the only one struggling here?
- When will the extreme temptation subside?
- What's the big deal about sex anyway?
- Who's out there to hold me accountable?
- How can I stop the cycle?

Who Moved the Goalpost? The Team Huddle is coming to your area. You'll leave the huddle and hit the playing field of life with a whole new game plan.

Who Moved the Goalpost?

THE TEAM HUDDLE

On the playing field of sexual integrity . . .

Which Guy Are You?

"Powerful advice!"
—Michael Ross, nationally recognized editor

"Lust is the #1 challenge facing Christian men . . . Bob reveals practical strategies to help in the war . . ."
—Clay Crosse, singer/songwriter

"There's nothing like this out there."
—Tony, 19 years old

Who Moved the Goalpost?
Is A Pure Freedom Program

Until 1974, the NFL's field goalpost was right on the goal line instead of at the back of the end zone as it is today. Sometimes when we're rushing around on the playing field of life, the temptation distracts us and . . . bammmm . . . you're nose deep in the goalpost of lust.

Can you identify?

There is hope. Who Moved the Goalpost? The Team Huddle is a high-contact event that'll revolutionize your view of sexual integrity. Bob Gresh will teach you seven winning strategies in the sexual integrity game plan. And would you believe he'll do it doing crazy stuff like playing Maul Ball?! In the heat of the games, you'll discover answers to vital questions such as:

- Am I the only one struggling here?
- When will the extreme temptation subside?
- What's the big deal about sex anyway?
- Who's out there to hold me accountable?
- How can I stop the cycle?

Who Moved the Goalpost? The Team Huddle is coming to your area. You'll leave the huddle and hit the playing field of life with a whole new game plan.